Navigating Oz

Gaining the Heart, Brain, and Courage to Invest

WYNDON A. HIBLER

Edited by: April D. Thompson - adrthompson@gmail.com
Cover and Interior design: Vanessa Mendozzi - www.vanessamendozzidesign.com
Images used under licence "Shutterstock.com"

ISBN 978-0-9978876-0-0 (paperback)
ISBN 978-0-9978876-1-7 (ebook)

Available from Amazon.com, CreateSpace.com, and other retail outlets

Disclaimer
This book gives general guidance in understanding the market place. You should
consult a financial advisor for personal advice. Investments are subject to losses.
Investors must use prudence when investing the financial market.

Contents

From the Author

With all the information on the internet, I have been asked why I am writing this book. The answer is simple. If someone did an internet search on any investment topic, they would get thousands of responses. It is difficult to gain an understanding of fragmented information. This book is written to give:

- Beginners an understanding of the financial markets;
- Novices a refresher of how to navigate the market;
- Experienced investors insight on how to better manage their resources.

Each group has different challenges on their financial journey. One size does not fit all. However, guidance will help investors avoid major pitfalls. So, as you read this book, keep these points in mind:

- Seek to own first what others will want later.
- Don't be too emotionally tied to material things that hold value that others are willing to buy.
- Fear and greed are the driving factors of the market. Knowledge and education are the balancing agents.
- There is a difference between knowledge and education. Knowledge is what you know while education is what you have learned or unlearned.
- Wisdom is a combination of knowledge, education, and experience.
- The only way to get experience is by doing it.

Wyndon

Introduction

"Lions, tigers, and bears, oh my!" Many are familiar with this popular phrase from L. Frank Baum's The Wonderful Wizard of Oz. The book's main character, Dorothy, found herself on a journey of self-exploration and trial and error, with help from some unlikely friends. For many, the world of investing can seem similar to Dorothy's experience in Oz. However, some may be unsure about whom to seek for help along their financial journey. Lack of investment knowledge, general fear of losing money or a lack of motivation can be deterrents. What if Dorothy didn't have the desire and motivation to return to Kansas? What happens when an individual has no desire and motivation to take care of their own financial well-being? That person will find themselves stranded in Oz, a long way from the desired destination.

When Dorothy awakened in Oz, she knew immediately where she wanted to be. While she didn't declare her motivation until the very end, her entire journey was singularly focused. A motivation declaration is the one phrase or thought that elicits excitement. Dorothy was clear about her motivation declaration. ("There's no place like home! There's no place like home!") Are you clear about what motivates you? What are your motivation declarations? If you don't have one, start with this: "There's nothing like financial freedom! There's nothing like financial freedom!"

The goal of this book is to:
- Explore the psychology of money
- Understand the products and vehicles of the market place
- Develop investment strategies

Dorothy traveled down the Yellow Brick Road with Tin Woodman, Scarecrow and Cowardly Lion, who sought a heart, brain and courage, respectively. The traveling companions on your financial journey are Money Psychology (Heart), Financial Tools (Brain), and Execution (Courage). Money Psychology deals with the relationship with money. It is the basis of risk taking or risk aversion. Financial Tools include the instruments you need to build your investment plan; it is the core knowledge that increases your understanding of the financial world. Finally, Execution shows how to put your plan to work.

Motivation Declaration

Motivation Declaration is that one thought or phrase that gets you going. We have multiple motivators that match different aspects of our lives. For example, the desire to be loved, have a family or find stability might be motivators to get married. The aspiration to have a better way of life may be the motivator to get an education and work hard. Motivation Declarations can be long-term or short-term focused. What motivates you?

Many people have desires and aspirations, but fail to activate them. So they can't begin their journey. It is more than identifying something that motivates or drive you. You have to own and declare it. Sometimes situations will force you to declare a motivation.

My Graduation

Going into my senior year, my parents decided to move to Charlotte, NC because of my stepfather's job. I decided to stay in Memphis to complete my senior year of high school. My goal was to graduate and go to Charlotte for the summer.

Graduation night turned from an ecstatic moment to one of dismay and sadness. Graduates were told to pick up their diplomas after the ceremonies. When names were called, mine was skipped. So, I asked the guidance counselor what happened. She told me I needed to see her at school the next day.

When I met with the guidance counselor, she told me I would have to attend summer school. I did not understand. She told me that while I had the hours to graduate, I did not have a major and two minors. My mind was blown. So many thoughts ran through my head. As she walked out of the room, she handed me a form and told me summer school would start in about two weeks. I left stunned! I was angry and wanted to cry as I drove down a hill from the school toward a stop sign. At that stop sign, my motivational declaration kicked in. "I will leave with my diploma today!"

I returned to school and asked to meet with the principal, Mr. Hunter. He knew me well; after all I was on the mock trial team, chess team, part of the basketball team and in advanced classes. By the time Mr. Hunter showed up, I was visibly upset. My parents had moved away and I decided to stay behind to finished my senior year of high school.

Mr. Hunter and I spoke for a few minutes. I could see the level of concern he had for me. He told me to wait a few minutes as he went to talk with the guidance counselor. When he returned, he explained the situation. He apologized for the confusion, as he told me what happened. Usually, students are required to have a major and two minors. I actually had two majors and a minor because I studied computer programming, technical drafting and French. He further explained that not many students have two majors. He again apologized as he handed me my diploma.

While my ultimate goal was to get to Charlotte that summer and prepare for college, short-term obstacles hampered it. My motivation declaration to leave school with my diploma started a chain reaction. Just like Dorothy, I found someone on my path to help me. I got what I needed to get to where I wanted to be. I ultimately completed my undergraduate and graduate studies.

Summary

- A motivation declaration is one phrase or thought that gets you excited.

- Your motivation declaration will help you overcome the fear or other obstacles that may be in search for value.

- Don't be afraid to ask for help on your journey.

Money Psychology

Who taught you about money? What did they teach you?

A person's relationship with money can be traced back to their adolescent years. Experience also plays a critical role in forming a person's viewpoint of money, how it works and how to use it. Money habits of savers and spenders more than likely formed from behavior learned or developed as young adults.

Research on generational attitudes and viewpoints of money show that each generation is influenced by the previous and shaped by the prevailing socioeconomic climate. While all individuals in a generation may not have the same characteristics, as a group they have similar behaviors. Here is an outline of the generations and some of their characteristics and behaviors:

Generational Influence on Money Psychology[1]

Mature/Silent Generation 1927 – 1945
- Post-war
- Marriage was for life, no out of wedlock children

---

1 Source: "Six Living Generations in America" by Dr. Jill Novak and "Generations and Money", TD Ameritrade Study

- Disciplined, self-sacrificing, cautious
- Managed income/expenses to live within means
- Retirement meant living final years in peace

Baby Boomers 1945 –1964

- The "Me" Generation
- Divorce rates increased and were considered more tolerable
- Self-righteous and self-centered
- Used credit to purchase immediately
- Women increasingly entered the workforce
- Household income increased
- More positive about hierarchal structure and tradition
- Generated enough income to live comfortably
- Retirement is more about enjoying life after children and more exploring

Generation X 1965 – 1980

- "Latch-Key" Kids
- Entrepreneurial
- Raised during the transitional technology era – written knowledge to digital based systems
- Want it now and heavy in debt
- Individualistic
- Cautious, skeptical, unimpressed with authority, self-reliant
- Reducing personal debt

Generation Y 1981 – 2000

- 9/11 Generation
- Nurtured by omnipresent parents,
- Feel enormous academic pressure
- Prefer digital literacy
- Prefer to work in teams
- Been told they are special and expect to be treated special

- Do not live to work. Prefer a more relaxed work environment
- Managing income/expenses to live within means

Millennials Born after 2000
- Record number of births in 2006 – almost half Hispanic
- Will be larger than the Baby Boomer Generation
- Already account for a significant amount of dollars in annual spend
- The cell phone generation
- KGOY – Kids Growing Older Younger
- Know what they want and how to get it

Culture and family relationships impact a person's money psychology. A 2010 research study conducted by Amia Barnea, Henrik Cronqvist and Stephan Siegel found that genes among fraternal and identical twins contributed to a difference of about one third of certain investment behaviors. Are you conservative or do you get really excited when taking on risk? Do you live for the moment? Do you view money as power and prestige or simply a means to an end? Do you like buying things or do you like the thought of having cash in the bank? Whatever your disposition is towards money, your genetic makeup and life experiences helped shape it.

Money management is impacted by one's mental disposition about money. Your disposition is also shaped by the culture of the family, socioeconomic interactions, and generational perspectives. Individuals born and raised during the Great Depression era generally were more conservative with their finances than their liberal-spending, baby-boomer offspring. While Generation X experienced a long, steady growth in the economy, both Generation Y and Millennials faced one of the worst economic climates since the Great Depression. The impact of this experience has been significant and will shape future generations.

Money psychology is rooted in lessons learned and life experiences. However, dispositions can be changed. It begins with your motivational declaration and then understanding your relationship with money. This relationship is based on fear and greed, perceived and real power of money and understanding what money represents.

A twenty-five cents lesson about life

In the summer of 1971, 25 cents could purchase a soda, Twinkies and chips. I was 6 years old and my great-grandmother, Mary Garner, was my keeper. We called her "Big Mama." She was 5' 7" and in her mid-seventies. One afternoon while I played in her front room, I found a quarter. I thought to myself: I could go to the store and get something. The store was right up the street and I had gone by myself before. So, I knew Big Mama would let me go.

"Big Mama, can I go to the store and get me something?"
"Where did you get money?"
"I found it in the front room," I said proudly.
"No!" She said sternly, "That's not your money; that's my money, in my house. Now, give me my money."

And she took the quarter from me. I was hurt, so I went back into the front room to cry, but I got over it. A week or two later, as I played at Big Mama's house again, I found another quarter. This time I went to her.

"Big Mama, is this your quarter? I found it in the front room."
"Yes, I must have lost it when I was cleaning up this morning. But you can keep it."

Later that day, she even let me go to the store. That summer, I found several more quarters in Big Mama's house. All of which she allowed me to keep.

Six years later, Big Mama talked to me about the summer of 1971. I'm not sure, but I believe she may have known it would be the last time I would see her. She talked about how quickly I caught on to the value of respecting other's property. She wanted to make sure that I learned the lessons she was trying to teach me over the years.

The lessons were not about the purchasing power of 25 cents, playing in Big Mama's house or going to the store. The lessons were about honesty with the resources we find during the journey through life. Most importantly, Big Mama's lessons were about being honest with oneself. Honesty is the foundation of our stewardship. The hardest person to be honest with is oneself, but it is one of the most important traits in life.

Dorothy was honest with herself on her quest to get back to Kansas. She was lost, fearful of the journey and needed help. As you read this book, you will have to assess yourself. It will require you to be honest with yourself, overcome fears and determine if you need help.

Summary

- Everyone has a relationship with money that can be traced back to adolescence.

- The relationship with money can be positive or negative.

- We are not bound by our early experiences with money. We have the power to change.

The Fear of Money

Chrometophobia is a big word that simply means the fear of money. It is an abnormal and persistent fear of money. Sufferers experience undue anxiety about money, even though they realize their fear is irrational. They worry that they might mismanage money or that money might live up to its reputation as "the root of all evil." Every person's experience with money is not as extreme, but there are many individuals whose money disposition can lead to chrometophobia. The fear of money is the basis for risk aversion. People who are risk averse are fearful of losing money and avoid investing in risky ventures. However, all investments have some level of risk. Therefore, risk aversion should be thought of as a way to take minimum risk for a minimum return on an investment.

Two human motivators are fear and greed. Fear is the motivator with which we have the most exposure. Real and perceived fears are often passed from generation to generation. You may be familiar with the following:

- Fear of failure
- Fear of dark places
- Fear of losing money

While we should take precautions when dealing with failure, dark places and even the investment market, too much fear can be worse than no fear.

While fear is openly communicated, greed is sometimes cloaked in the idea of your biggest dream or greatest desire. Too much fear as well as too much greed can have almost the same effect. You can find yourself off your desired path. Risk is the fear of loss. Loss can be produced from too much fear as well as too much greed.

Just as fear and greed go together, so do risk and reward. As previously mentioned, most investments have some level of risk. We invest our time, talents, money and other resources. We invest for some type of reward, but our decision to invest has to consider the potential for loss (risk). The risks of not getting a degree or losing that job are real possibilities.

Whether we are aware or not, we manage the balance of risk and reward every day. The balancing act of walking, driving our cars or taking a flight all show our decision to take on risk for some type of reward. We consciously and unconsciously manage this risk/reward paradigm. Risk management can be viewed as how we manage this fear of loss.

In general, we can:
- Accept the risk and do the activity,
- Find a way to lessen the risk and do the activity, or
- Avoid the activity thus avoid the risk.

The fear of money and the fear of taking risks are rooted in money psychology. Our socioeconomic background helps to shape what we view as risky activities. Some people believe using any debt to buy things is too risky. On the other hand, some people elect to use debt to leverage their way of life. Regardless of which group you fall into or between, the fear of loss and the management of risk is something to which we are exposed. We can manage the risks in life. We can overcome the fears we have about money. We can change.

Dorothy had many fears as she began her journey. Her view on life had been shaped by the culture she experienced on a Kansas farm. She had to decide to accept the risks to reach her ultimate reward of getting home. She experienced many enlightening and challenging obstacles during her travels down the yellow brick road. However, she overcame her fears.

Summary

- The fear of money, chrometophobia, is the basis for risk aversion.

- Risk aversion is the avoidance of loss.

- Every event has some level of risk.

- Risk can be accepted, mitigated, or avoided.

- Risk always comes before reward (except in the dictionary and a few arbitrage situations).

Change Management

It can take, on average, 90 days for a behavior to become a habit. Yet, it often can seem more like a lifetime. The subconscious imagery is one of the most powerful tools of the human mind. Once we imagine ourselves doing something, our subconscious craves it. Once we crave it, we seek it. The more we feed this subconscious imagery, the more we desire it in our consciousness. This applies to almost everything, including our money relationship, but habits can be changed.

Change management is an inside game. It isn't that something happens to us. What is important is how we respond. For example, if I pinched you, there are several things you can do: scream, pinch or hit me or do nothing. Consequently, if this occurred in front of an audience, the next person that I approach would be leery of me. They would expect to be pinched. This is an example of individual and group change management. The action to one or several individuals can impact the entire group.

These interactions and responses drive human behavior. An example of this is when a child falls. After the fall, the child tries to figure out what happened and how to respond to this event. If the adult runs to them with fear, the child starts crying immediately, regardless of the level of injury. If the adult tries consolation, the child starts crying. However, if the adult gets down to the child's level and asks the child if everything is okay, stands him/her up, the child probably will smile and continue playing.

Our initial way of asking for things, responding to events and interacting with others begins when we are young. We are also introduced to our money management behaviors when we are young. The spending, saving and investment habits that we employ today were developed at a young age. These habits are reinforced over time. By the time we become adults, they drive our decision making process, but habits can be changed.

There are behaviors that are introduced and adopted. For example, we are taught our studying, dieting and worshiping habits. Some behaviors develop as we grow and experience new and different life events. The decisions to ride a bike weekly, exercise daily or consume alcohol on weekends are behaviors that can become habits. When we no longer like an activity or behavior, we can abandon it. Habits can be changed.

Behaviors are not formed. Behaviors are introduced, adopted and practiced. They can be selected, changed or abandoned. Habits represent repetitive behavior. As it relates to money management, habits are behaviors you practice day-to-day. If you want to change your behavior consider these three things: self-observation, conscious selection and practice.

Self-observation is the act of becoming aware of one's own actions and reactions to events. You have practiced behaviors all your life that impact your relationship with money. Self-observation is challenging. It can cause significant frustration and pain. However, self-awareness in different money management events can help you make better financial decisions. Give yourself 30 or 60 days to observe how you respond to the following events:

- How do you feel when you get paid?
- How do you feel when you hear or see a sale?
- How do you feel when you pay with cash versus a card?
- How do you feel when a friend buys something you like?

- How would you feel if you won $1,000? $100,000? $1 million?
- How would you feel if you lost $100? $10,000? $100,000?
- Do you have buyer's remorse with large purchases?
- Do you buy things then return them?
- Do you get angry when you can't buy something?
- Do you pick up coins when you see them on the ground?

These are just a few self-observation questions. Most of them are emotional questions. As previously mentioned, the subconscious imagery is one of the most powerful tools of the human mind. The craving for things has an emotional connection. The goal of self-observation is to know and understand oneself. It helps you discover what influence money has on you and your ability to control yourself. We need the ability to control ourselves before we can control money.

Once you have observed your behaviors with money, you can determine which habits to keep and which to abandon. After all, some learned behaviors may be helpful. At this point, you begin to make conscious money management behavior selections and determine what new behaviors to adopt. The motivational declaration plays a huge part here. Dorothy's motivational declaration caused her to adopt new behaviors. She learned to think differently, have courage and demonstrate her love. The following examples describe some money management behaviors:

- Setting money aside from each paycheck – retirement and saving
- Living within your financial means – after you have set money aside
- Increasing your financial acumen – never stop learning
- Buying things that hold or increase in value

Self-observation and conscious behavior selection represent the first two stages of change management. The final stage is practice. You practiced the behaviors introduced when you were young until they become habits. New behaviors must be practiced as well, but it can be challenging. Putting a timeframe on when a behavior becomes a habit is extremely challenging.

However, the effectiveness and consistency of financial activities can be measured. The effectiveness of a financial activity is based on contribution, growth and time. Once you determine the activity's effectiveness, then you can move to consistency of doing the activity. For example, you have a financial motivational declaration to save 10 percent of your salary. Your company matches up to 6 percent contribution to retirement accounts. You elect to contribute 6 percent to your retirement account. Your contribution of 6 percent and your company's match put your total savings at 12 percent. That is an effective activity that matches the behavior of setting money aside. Maintaining this activity every year shows consistency.

The Power of the Penny

How many times have you walked past a penny without picking it up? You probably can't count the number of times. Have you ever asked yourself why you don't take the time to pick it up? Our society has created a "more-is-best" mentality. If it is not big money, then it's worthless. Today's society focuses on instant gratification. However, it still takes 100 pennies to make a dollar, and it still takes 100 dollar bills to make $100.

In regard to the penny and money psychology, there are a few things we must realize. We don't have to "pinch" every penny, but we should respect the penny. It is the basis of value exchange in our country. We deal in dollars and cents. If you begin to manage the cents better, the dollars will soon be under your control. The penny's power is undeniable.

The stock market works in penny increments. When you are reading the markets or looking at a stock, the spread between the bid and offer is in pennies. In order for a stock to move from $10 per share to $20 per share, it moves in one-cent increments. Companies report earnings per share in pennies (cents). However, if you were to multiply any of the figures by a large number of shares, you get a large dollar value.

A bank convinces checking account depositors to keep the change from each debit card transaction in a separate account. The bank agrees to pay a nominal interest rate. The depositors on average save about $250 a year in the new account. Millions of depositors add up to a large dollar value. The bank can then make loans against those dollars at a higher interest rate.

A city, county or state taxes citizens 0.082 percent per thousand on the assessed value of their home. The average house has an assessed value of $160,000. So, taxes due for the year is $1,312. But, there are thousands or millions homeowners paying similar bills. That works out to be a big dollar value.

These examples sound big, but they start with a small concept: the power of the penny. So, while we believe that we should focus on big dollars, most companies and institutions start by focusing on the pennies. We should begin to respect the power of the penny and how it impacts our way of life.

Summary

- Change management is more than how we use the coins in our pockets.

- The challenge is how we change what we subconsciously crave.

- Pennies have more impact in our society than we acknowledge.

- We should learn to respect the power of the penny.

What is Money?

Money does not exist. I know you use cash, checks, credit and debit cards. When you look in your accounts, you see what is thought of as money.

So if money does not exist, what does? Value. By definition, value is an amount, as of goods and services, considered a fair and suitable equivalent for something else. It also represents worth in usefulness or importance to the possessor, utility or merit such as the value of an education. What is seen as money is really a placeholder for value. It represents value created through work, transferred from another source or accrued over time.

Money is a representation of value, but value does not represent money. Value is a perceived attribute. What is considered valuable to one individual may be worthless to another. Often, some individuals value things long before others see the same value. This change in attitude is what creates value.

Money is a tool. Its primary use is value exchange. It is the amount someone is paid for working. It can be the official medium of exchange, such as a commodity like gold. It can be the unofficial medium of exchange that can be used to purchase goods and services. It is a placeholder of value.

Money has positive and negative energy. Because money is a tool used to exchange value, it is meant to flow. Anything that has continuous flow creates a current. Currents create energy. All energy sources have positive and negative attributes. If money is not flowing, there is no current; thus, no energy is created. In other words, if value isn't created, no money is being exchanged. If no money is being exchanged, there is no energy source and everything stops.

Finally, money has perceived and real power. If you ask people what they would do with their lives if money was not an issue, you will hear all types of dreams and goals. People perceive a lack of money as the element that stops them from pursuing their dreams. The perceived value of money is what people believe money can do in their lives.

The real power of money is what you can exchange for it and what can be purchased with it. However, it comes with a cost. Economic forces erode the real power of money over time. Risk, inflation and taxes diminish the real power of money.

In the investment world, value can be found in many different forms, such as real estate, commodities, precious metals and financial instruments. Over the years, money has taken many forms in exchanging value. It has been represented by everything from fruit and vegetables, grain, rocks and precious metals. Hence, the theory that money does not exist. While it takes on different forms, its sole purpose is to store and transfer value.

Money Attributes

- Various methods of exchange: bartering, precious metal, currency
- Exchange of value
- Tool used to settle obligations
- Perceived and real power
- Positive and negative energy

Summary

- Money doesn't exist. Don't chase money. Search for value.

- Money is a representation of value, but value doesn't represent money.

- Money is a tool and can take many forms.

- Money has positive and negative energy.

- The perceived power of money is what people think they can do with money in their lives.

- Economic forces erode the real power of money.

My first stock purchase

I had been working at Interstate/Johnson Lane (IJL), a regional brokerage firm, for three years. I initially worked part-time in operations before moving to full-time employment as I worked my way through college.

My first experience with the investment process was my company-sponsored retirement account, or 401(k). I did not make much money, but I liked the thought of the company matching what I contributed. I contributed six percent. I did not know what I was doing, so I relied on guidance from a friend and put most of my money in growth-type funds that the company offered. It was confusing, challenging and scary to figure out. With some help, I began to understand it, and it proved to be a good thing. My consistent savings and company match, combined with the growth of the investments, gave me a nice pre-tax savings for my future retirement.

But it did not stop there. A friend and co-worker encouraged me to buy a stock. I had never purchased stocks, so I didn't know what to do. She explained the steps, including how to open an account, research companies and make a selection.

Opening the brokerage account was a little scary. I was given a long form to complete, and I was unsure how to answer many of the questions. Because we worked at a brokerage firm, it was a little easier for me since I knew the broker.

My friend showed me an IJL Recommendations list that contained the analysts' views on the companies they followed and rated. Recommendations were either BUY, HOLD or SELL. I researched and chose Birmingham Steel Corporation (BIR) for my first purchase. The analyst rated it a BUY, and it traded at $10 per share, with a price target of $25. I called the broker who opened my account and bought 100 shares, because my friend advised me to buy a minimum of 100 shares, also known as a "block." I thought it was a lot, but I did it. I stood to lose $1,070, after buying $1,000 worth of stocks and being charged a $70 brokerage commission. The broker told me I had five days to deposit the money into the account to settle the trade.

I was eager for the stock to reach $25 per share. My friend informed me that stock maturation is a long-term process, which meant between 24 to 36 months. "36 months? 36 months! Wait, that's three years!" I shouted, "You did not tell me I had to wait three years!" "Wyndon," she calmly replied, "that is the definition of long-term investment. It may or may not reach that target within the timeframe. Be patient."

I tried to be patient. I watched that stock everyday. Day after day it stayed at $10. Then one day, I looked at the price, and it had decreased to $8. I became nervous and thought I had lost money. "Calm down, Wyndon," my friend said. "The stock may fluctuate. Be patient!"

For three weeks, I did not look at the stock. My friend gave me a report on BIR that showed that the company had exceeded earnings estimates for the quarter. The stock price increased to $12 per share. In one year, the stock grew to $18 per share. I eventually sold my 100 shares of BIR at $32 per share. I was fortunate that my first purchase was a good experience. I learned a lot and my confidence increased.

After completing my undergraduate degree, I became an equity analyst assistant in IJL's Research Department. I actually became one of the analysts who covered Birmingham Steel, my first stock purchase.

Investment Tools

Whether she knew it or not, Dorothy had several tools in Oz. She had the yellow brick road that gave direction. She had signposts along her journey to Oz. Finally, she had her shoes that ultimately were used to get home. Investment tools will help you reach your goal of finding value in the market place.

Before we go further, clarification between finance and investment should be explained. Often people ask if I can help with their finances. Upon questioning, it becomes evident they are asking for investment help. There is a clear distinction between investing and financing. Investing is the decision of what to buy and when to buy it. Financing is how you will pay for it.

Let's say you decide to buy a $200,000 house. You determine that you want to buy it by the end of the year. Next, you go to a bank to get a loan for 80 percent of the value of the house, and you put down 20 percent. You get the loan for 30 years with a 5 percent interest payment. This is a financing decision. The primary assumption going forward is the financing decision (you got the money) is confirmed. We will focus on the investment decision.

Our goal is to search for value. Money is the primary holder of value. It can be used to exchange value. In our economy, it represents value held in savings accounts, money market accounts or other money depository avenues. It is the method by which we exchange value in our society. Investment Tools consist of investment vehicles and investment products. There are a multitude of investment vehicles. However, there are only three types of monetary investment products: cash, stocks and bonds.

Investment Products

Cash

As previously stated, money is a storehouse of value. Cash is money in the form of bills or coins. It is the currency that is used for immediate payment for goods or services. Sometimes it is viewed as short-term assets that can be exchanged for or converted into ready money. Cash is the least risky investment product to hold. However, the reward is sometimes the lowest. Cash can be held in a multitude of investment vehicles and can readily be moved from account to account. Cash is the only investment product that can be carried by the individual. Because of this flexibility, it can be used instantly to settle obligations between parties. When held in investment vehicles, it can generate a return based on the prevailing market interest rates.

- Money in the form of bills or coins (currency)
- Immediate payment for goods or services in currency
- To exchange for or convert into ready money
- Extremely liquid

Bonds

A bond is an investment product that represents a binding agreement or covenant. It represents a promise or obligation by which one is bound. It is a certificate of debt issued by a government or corporation, which guarantees payment of the original investment plus interest by a specified future date. There are several types of bonds: Corporate, Government and Agency, Municipal, Mortgage-backed, Asset-backed, Collateralized Debt and Funding.

Bondholders are lenders to the company, local, state or federal entity. The entity pays interest to the lender to compensate for the loan. The expectation is that the government or company will repay the loan plus interest. The term of the loan can be as short as three months and as long as 30 years. The interest paid on the bond is based on the prevailing market interest rate, as well as the credit profile of the borrower. So, the bondholder risks the repayment of the original investment, receipt of the interest payment, impact of the current interest rate market and future reinvestment risks.

Bonds were issued in two forms: Bearer and Registered. Bearer bonds were pieces of paper without the owner's name on it. The attached interest coupons could be clipped and taken to the bank for payment. This increased the likelihood of the bonds being stolen without recourse. Some bearer bonds may still be outstanding because of their maturity date. However, trust agents no longer issue them. Registered bonds have the owner's name on the bond and on the trustee agent's records. Some bondholders demand to have physical bonds delivered to them. Holding physical bonds sometimes slows transaction processing times. Since the 1990s, more bonds have been purchased in the book entry form. The purchaser doesn't receive a physical bond; they are listed as owner with the trustee agent.

Bonds carry more risks than cash, and there is an expectation of enough reward to justify the investment. Sometimes investors will use bonds as a short-term replacement of cash because of the higher interest rate. Bonds are usually sold in increments of $1,000 or $5,000, depending on the issuer. The interest rate represents the amount the holder will receive annually for holding the bond.

There is an inverse relationship between interest rates and a bond's market value. An older bond's market value will fluctuate based on the prevailing market interest rate. If the new bond has a higher interest rate, the older bond's market value will decrease. If the new bond has a lower interest rate, the older bond's value will increase.

U.S. Government bonds once were considered risk-free; payment of interest and the repayment of principal were assured. Thus, government bonds have been the basis for the pricing of many other investment instruments including municipal bonds, corporate bonds, mortgages, stocks and their derivatives.

For example, the United States Treasury issues two-year, five-year, 10-year and 30-year bonds that incorporate interest rates that are considered fair for the length of time to maturity. Accordingly, in normal markets, longer-term bonds will have higher interest rates than shorter-term bonds. A 30-year bond will have a higher interest rate than the 10-year, five-year and two-year bonds. If the economy struggles, investors will buy shorter-term bonds that can invert this relationship in bonds.

As previously mentioned, other types of financial products are based on government bonds. For example, mortgages were based on the 30-year bond interest rate. If the U.S., 30-year bond interest rate stood at 5 percent, the bank would start with that rate and add a percentage to it to create the mortgage rate. While mortgages were based on the 30- year bond, the average mortgage is paid off in 10 years. Thus, the 10-year rate is the bellwether for mortgage rates.

Bond Attributes
- A binding agreement or covenant; a promise or obligation by which one is bound.
- A certificate of debt issued by a government or corporation guaranteeing payment of the original investment plus interest by a

specified future date.
- Represents lenders to the company.
- Company pays interest to the lender to compensate for the loan.
- If the company goes under, lenders are the first to receive proceeds from the distribution of assets.

Below are grouping of bonds based on issuers and coupon characteristics.

TABLE 1 - BOND TYPES	
Bonds by issuer	**Bonds by coupon**
Corporate bond	Fixed rate bond
Government bond	Floating rate note
Municipal bond	Zero-coupon bond
	Inflation-indexed bond
	Commercial paper
	Perpetual bond

Common Stock

Common stock, the last type of monetary exchange, represents limited ownership in a company. The limited ownership reduces the investor's risk if the company goes out of business. Another name for common stock is equity. It is said a common stockholder has equity in the company. This means once all obligations are paid, the residuals, or net profits, go to the common shareholders. However, the company may reinvest this into the business. Some companies, on the other hand, pay out a portion of their earnings (profits) to shareholders in the form of a dividend. While common stock shareholders own an equity share of the business, they are always paid last. If the company goes under, shareholders are the last group to get proceeds from the distribution of assets. Key attributes of common stock include:

- Ordinary capital shares of a corporation, usually giving the owners

a vote.
- Represents limited ownership
- Some distribute earnings by paying dividends
- If the company goes under, these are the last people to get proceeds from the distribution of assets

Hybrids of investment products

There are three core investment products: cash, stocks, and bonds. However, investment companies have created mixtures, or hybrids, of these three investment products to serve a wider investment audience. These investments are derived from the core investment products. Three commonly used hybrids are mutual funds, exchanged-traded funds (ETFs) and options.

Mutual funds allow investors to pool their money and invest based on objectives of the fund's prospectus (brochure that gives details of the mutual fund). Every dollar in the mutual fund receives equal treatment regardless of the size of the investment. Professional investment managers make investment decisions based on extensive research. Because mutual funds are managed by professional investment managers, investors are charged annual management fees. An investor should thoroughly research the true cost of owning the fund, as other charges or fees may be associated with owning mutual funds.

The objective of a mutual fund is to reduce individual stock risk by using diversification. Diversification is investing in several different companies that behave differently with swings in the market place. Diversification can be based on sector, industry or capitalization. There are mutual funds that are based solely on cash, stock or bonds. Then, there are some that are a mixture of the three.

A mutual fund's value is measured as the Net Asset Value (NAV), or the fund's assets minus its liabilities. The value is set daily after the market closes and measured on a per-share basis.

An Exchange Traded Fund (ETF) is an investment product that tracks an index, a commodity, bonds or a basket of assets like an index fund. An ETF trades like a common stock on a stock exchange. These types of funds experience price changes throughout the day as they are bought and sold. ETFs have become an attractive alternative to mutual funds, because their daily trading volume is higher, and fees are lower than mutual fund shares. Unlike mutual funds, an ETF does not have its net asset value (NAV) calculated at the end of the day.

Another investment hybrid is an option. It is a contract sold by one party (option writer) to another party (option holder). The contract gives the holder the right to buy (call) or sell (put) a security or other financial asset at an agreed-upon price (the strike price) during a certain period of time or on a specific date (exercise date). One option typically represents 100 shares of the underlying security. Call Options give the right, but not the obligation to buy at certain price, so the buyer would want the stock to go up. Put Options give the right, but not the obligation to sell at a certain price, so the buyer would want the stock to go down.

Valuation

While money can take on many forms, its sole purpose is to store and transfer value. We have spoken a lot about money; however, bonds and stocks are other tools that are used to store and transfer value. They represent the current and perceived future value of the company. Therefore, it is the perceived value of the company that drives the price of the company's bonds or stock. The valuation, an estimation of what a company is worth, is derived from examining the key elements of the company's financial history to determine how well they run the business. These key elements are found on the company's balance sheet and income statement. Companies are considered live entities. As such, the balance sheet can be viewed as the body of the company and the income statement as the blood. Valuation of the company examines the health of the company and how well it operates. The company's financial history helps determine if it is viable to own the company or hold the company's debt. There are a lot of analyses that can be performed; however, answering these six questions can help determine if the investor can find value in a company.

1. Does the company have a lot of debt?
2. How well does the company manage it resources?
3. Is the company making a profit?
4. Does the investor get paid (interest or dividend)?
5. Are we paying too much for the stock or bond?
6. How does the company compare to it peers and the overall market?

These key calculations and others used to evaluate companies can be found in the Valuation Table in the appendix. Let's examine two measures that are emphasized in the market place: price-to-earnings and beta.

Price-to-Earnings Ratio or P/E Ratio measures the relationship between the company's earnings and the current or future stock price. It is derived by dividing the stock price by the company's earnings per share. Historical calculations measure how much investors paid for reported earnings. Current calculations measure how much investors are willing to pay for future earnings. With the P/E calculation the investor can determine the expected future price of a stock. For example: ABC stock currently trades at $15. Its historical P/E Ratio is 15x where "x" is the sign for multiplication. Next year, if the company's earnings are $2 per share, the expected price next year would be $30.

Not only does the P/E ratio give insight on a stock's future performance, it can also give insight into how a company's stock performs relative to other stocks as well as overall market sentiment. If ABC stock trades at 15x and XYZ stock trades at 10x future earnings and they both expect to earn $2.00 next year, we would say that ABC stock is more expensive than XYZ stock. The investor would have to pay $30 per share this year to own ABC stock earnings of $2.00 next year. On the other hand, the investor would have to pay $20 per share to own the XYZ stock next year's earnings.

Historically, the average P/E ratio of all stocks in the market is 13x. So if a stock has a P/E ratio of 13x, it is considered fairly valued compared to the overall market. If it has a P/E ratio below 13x, it is considered inexpensive compared to the overall market. If the stock has a P/E ratio above 13x, it is considered expensive compared to the overall market. The market average P/E ratio changes over time, but the relative value definition is consistent.

While P/E ratios can help determine expected future value and relative cost of ownership, Beta give insight to how a stock moves with the market. Beta is a statistical measure. Every security has a calculated beta. If a security has a beta equal to 1, its price movement is in line with the overall market. If the security has a beta less than 1, its price movement is less impacted by movements of the overall market. If the security has a beta greater than 1, its price movement will be impacted more by movements of the overall market.

Investment Vehicles

Investment vehicles are the accounts that hold the investment products. While there are three basic investment products, there are multiple investment vehicles. Some vehicles can only hold one investment product (cash), while others can hold all three as well as their derivatives.

Bank-side Vehicles

Checking, savings accounts, CD holding accounts and secured and unsecured loan accounts are the primary types of bank side vehicles. The only investment product they can hold is cash. Most bank-side vehicles are insured by the Federal Deposit Insurance Corporation (FDIC). FDIC insures most of the nation's commercial banks. To belong to the FDIC, a bank must meet certain standards and agree to let both federal and state agencies regularly examine its books. Member banks pay insurance fees to maintain the FDIC's Bank Insurance Fund. Deposits at those banks are insured for up to $100,000.

Brokerage Vehicles

Bank-side vehicles can only hold one type of investment product. Primarily these types of accounts are used to settle obligations and save. There are other types of accounts targeted for investment purposes. Brokerage Vehicles include but are not limited to the following: 401(k) plans, Individual Retirement Account (IRA), Brokerage Account and Insurance Holding Accounts. It's important to know that these accounts may lose value, are not FDIC insured or bank guaranteed.

The investment products held in these accounts may lose value. The FDIC only insures checking and savings accounts. Investment product performance is not guaranteed.

However, the Securities Investor Protection Corp. (SIPC) insures many types of investments held at stock brokerage firms. Neither a government agency nor a regulatory authority, the SIPC is a nonprofit, membership corporation, funded by its member securities broker-dealers. If the brokerage house fails and does not have enough securities or funds to settle all claims, the rest will be met by the SIPC—up to $500,000 per customer—including $100,000 for cash accounts. It is imperative to note; investment losses are not covered by the SIPC.

Qualified Retirement Plans

A Qualified Retirement Plan (QRP) is a type of retirement plan established by employers for the benefit of their employees. There are two types of Qualified Retirement Plans: defined benefit and defined contribution. Defined benefit plans give employees a guaranteed payout and places investment risk on the employer. The employee has no say in the investment decisions of the plan. A traditional pension plan is an example of a defined benefit plan.

A Defined Contribution plan allows the employee to contribute a portion of their pre-taxed income toward their retirement. An employee can deposit up to 15 percent of their gross salary, often with the company matching a portion of the employee's contributions. The employee can select from a defined selection of stock, bond or money market mutual funds. The employer may also give the employee the option to invest in the company's stock. Income tax is deferred on the amount the employee puts into the plan until it is withdrawn.

Withdrawals from the account may be made without penalty after 59 1/2. A penalty of 10 percent of the principal is assessed if the account is withdrawn before age 59 1/2. The 401(k) and 403(b) Plans are examples of Defined Contribution Plans.

Individual Retirement Account (IRA)

Individual Retirement Accounts (IRAs) help self-employed and small business employees contribute to their retirement. An IRA is a personal, tax-deferred retirement account that a self-employed person can establish with a deposit up to $2,000 per year. Withdrawals from the account may be made without penalty after 59 1/2. Prior to this age there is usually a 10 percent (of principal) penalty. Most people are encouraged to roll their employer-sponsored plans into an IRA when they leave the company. IRAs are sometimes called Self-Directed IRA because the individual determines the investment choices.

Roth IRA

A retirement plan named for Senator William Roth, Jr., former chair of the Senate Finance Committee, the ROTH IRA plan allows an annual contribution of $2,000 per individual or $4,000 per couple. If the investment is held for five years, the money earned is not taxed if used to purchase your first house or after age 59 ½. Contributions to a Roth IRA are not tax deductible. The traditional IRA and the Roth IRA plans can hold cash, stocks, bonds, mutual funds, ETFs and real estate investment trusts.

Brokerage Account

A brokerage account is an arrangement between a licensed brokerage firm and an investor that allows the investor to deposit funds and place investment orders. The brokerage firm acts as an agent for the investor. The account is a record of all transactions in which the investor has been involved. The investor will receive statements disclosing monthly transactions, current positions, and cash balances. Almost all types of investment products can be held in a brokerage account.

Annuities

An annuity is an insurance vehicle that pays out income and can be used as part of a retirement strategy. It is a contract between the investor and an insurance company in which the investor makes a lump sum payment or a series of payments. In return, the investor will receive regular disbursements immediately or at some point in the future. Annuities are a popular choice for investors who want to receive a steady income stream in retirement. Two common types of annuities are fixed and variable.

Fixed Annuity

A Fixed Annuity is an insurance vehicle in which the recipient regularly deposits money that will be paid out to the recipient or a designated beneficiary as income. Such annuities protect the person's principal, allow the annuitants to defer taxes on the interest, and exclude the income from any probate proceedings. The customer can potentially benefit from the effects of compounding by earning on the principal, the earnings and the money that otherwise would have been paid in taxes.

Variable Annuity

A Variable Annuity is an annuity contract which provides future payments to the holder (the annuitant), usually at retirement. The size of the payment depends on the performance of the portfolio's securities. Variable annuities allow the insured to choose how the premiums are invested among 10 to 25 funds. These funds are held in sub-accounts which allow the investor to decide what to invest in and how much of a risk to take. By allocating portions of the investment to different asset classes, it is possible to achieve a balance between risk and potential reward that is suitable for the investor's particular circumstances. However, the policy's cash value, along with the death benefit, can fluctuate depending on the performance of the chosen investment.

The Market

My first taxable job was a Front-End Customer Support Specialist at Giant's Food Market on Austin-Peay Highway in Memphis, TN. In others words, I was a grocery sacker. Back then, grocers only used paper bags. Minimum wage was $4.35, but the bulk of the money was made in tips. These guidelines helped me become a great grocery bagger:

- Respect the customer
- Make sure to keep cold food separate
- Double-sack meats
- Protect the bread and eggs
- Know how to load the car

The biggest secret I learned about being a good sacker and getting the best tips was to make sure the grocery cart rolled correctly! The wrong cart could:

- make it difficult keep up with the customer
- cause the cart to flip or damage the goods
- create a noise from the cart that irritates the customer or makes you look unprofessional.

The vehicle used to deliver things from one place to another may be more important than the products inside. The vehicle has to have the ability to protect its cargo.

Giant's later changed to Piggly Wiggly. Over the next year and a half, I not only sacked; I worked in both the produce and deli departments. I also stocked shelves on weekends. I learned the layout of the store pretty well.

Years later, one of my mentors in the financial world said: "It is not a stock market; it is a market of stocks!" For me the connection was clear. A market is a market. The stock market has some interesting comparisons to a supermarket.

We have explored the characteristics of the investment products: cash, stocks and bonds. We also talked about derivatives and alternative investments such as mutual funds and options. The next time you walk into your friendly, neighborhood supermarket consider these similarities. The first section you enter is the produce department. It contains grocery items with the shortest shelf life. Therefore, it must be replenished often. Cash has the same characteristics, because it is extremely short-lived and must constantly be replenished. It is usually the first thing one learns about when beginning to invest in the financial markets.

Now, when you walk down those aisles and see all those cans, boxes, bottles, and jars of goods, think of stock. As a matter of fact, supermarkets use the term stock when referring to products in the stores. You see rows and rows of stocks just like the financial streaming of stocks on the big boards on Wall Street.

Bonds are like the frozen section. Just like the items you buy and put in your freezer, bonds are items you buy for later consumption. The only difference is that bonds may pay interest while frozen foods just take up space in your freezer. Working in the deli is like being the manager of a mutual fund or hedge fund. They get paid to select items from produce (cash), shelves (stocks) and the freezer (bonds) to create something special for individuals to consume.

Finally, the investment vehicle is the food cart. It is imperative that the investment advisor ensures that the investment vehicle works correctly for the customer.

Summary

- There are only three types of monetary investment products: cash, stocks, and bonds. Cash is the most liquid. Bonds represent a loan to the company or entity. Stocks represent ownership in the company. There are multiple variations or derivatives based on these basic monetary products.

- Stocks and Bonds represent ownership or debtor relationship to a company. Investors determine this relationship by evaluating the company's health as well as it performance to its peers and the overall market.

- Investment vehicles are the accounts that hold the investment products. While there are various vehicles, they can be categorized by traditional bank-side and investment-side accounts. The primary difference between the two is that bank-side accounts can only hold cash, while investment-side accounts can hold all types of investment products.

- The financial markets are not much different than a supermarket.

Grouping of Companies

While my supermarket analogy seems simplistic, it should give a better understanding of the big picture. Cash, Stock, and Bonds are the products, and each has a specific purpose for those who need to raise funds, as well as those who want to invest their money. Thinking back to the supermarket analogy, the concept is that there is an order to the Financial Markets.

There are several markets where trading takes place:
- Stock market
- Bond market
- Futures market
- Foreign exchange market
- Commodity market
- Spot market
- Over-the-counter market (OTC)

NYSE, Euronext and the NASDAQ OMX are the largest exchanges in America and the world based on market capitalization and trade value. There are thousands of different companies in the stock markets. However, companies can be grouped based on similar characteristics and profiles. Three common group views of companies are Capitalization, Category and Sectors/Industries.

Grouping stocks by capitalization

Capitalization has several meanings, such as the accounting view of acquiring an asset, the sum of a company's financing sources (cash, stock and bond) or a company's market capitalization. Most investors focus on the market value to group stocks. In general terms, the grouping of stocks based on market capitalizations (Caps) can be defined as a company's stock price multiplied by the number of shares outstanding.

Mega Caps are companies with more than $200 Billion in market capitalization. Only a few companies fall into this group, and they are considered industry leaders.

Large Caps are companies whose values fall within $20 Billion and $200 Billion. Many well-known companies fall in this range. These companies are considered stable and secure.

Mid-Caps range from $2 Billion to $10 Billion. They are considered more volatile than mega and large cap companies. Growth companies make up a significant portion of mid-caps. They may not be industry leaders but may well be on the way.

Small-Caps don't have the same track record as mid to mega cap stocks. Their market capitalization falls between $300 million to $2 Billion. They offer the possibility of greater capital appreciation, but it comes with greater risk. They may not be as stable as mega, large or mid-caps. They may not have enough resources to last through downturns in their industry or the economy. They usually are new companies with no track record.

Micro-Caps are sometimes called penny stocks. Market capitalization falls between $50 million and $300 million. These stocks have similar upside and downside potential. They are considered speculative investments and carry significantly higher risk.

Nano-Caps have market capitalization below $50 million. They are the riskiest group to invest and the upside is limited. These stocks tend to trade on pink sheets or Over the Counter Bulletin Board (OTCBB).

These definitions and ranges are not set in stone. They may fluctuate depending on how the overall market is performing.

Grouping by categories

Stocks can be grouped into different categories: Blue Chips, Income, Growth, Value, Cyclical, and Defensive.

Blue Chips

Companies that are considered blue chips have sound financials and are well established. Their market values are in the billions and they are usually one of the top three companies in their sector. Most blue chip stocks have a history of paying stable or rising dividends for years if not decades. Their P/E ratio is often below the average as their fair value is reflected in the stock price. Because of the longevity and survival through different challenges, blue chip stocks are considered a safer investment than other types of stocks. They also tend to be household names.

Income Stocks

Income-paying stocks represent companies that pay an annual dividend. The dividend represents distribution of the company's profits. The dividend can be communicated in an absolute dollar amount that reflects the amount paid based on the number of shares owned. It can be communicated relative to the stock's dollar price or dividend yield.

Growth Stocks

A growth stock's price is expected to rise quickly because the issuing company is in an expanding industry or in the midst of some new and potentially popular product or service. Although in the long-term growth stocks outperform average stocks, they are riskier than average stocks because of their higher P/E ratios.

Value Stocks

A value stock trades at a price lower than its valuation. The P/E ratio is lower than its peer group. The dividend yield may be higher than its peers. A value investor expects the stock to outperform the market going forward as its price catches up. Value stocks are often found in the financial, capital goods and retail sectors.

Cyclical Stocks

Cyclical stocks move in and out of favor with their sector of the economy. Cyclical can mean seasonal or the economic period. They can make great investments if bought at the right time—or prove to be a disaster if purchased at the wrong time. Steel and oil companies are examples of cyclical stocks.

Defensive Stocks

Defensive stocks are identified by their performance during different economic cycles. They are considered stable companies that usually pay a good dividend. These companies usually offer products or services that are considered necessities. In down economic cycles (recessions and depressions), defensive stocks tend to outperform the market. However, during expansion periods, they will underperform the market. Utility companies are examples of defensive stocks.

Sectors and industries

In the previous two sections we talked about grouping of companies by market capitalization and investment categories. Many companies have moved up and down the market capitalization spectrum as well as the investment category bucket. A more stable grouping of companies is by sectors and industry standards. While similar, sectors and industry grouping have a very clear and distinct difference.

Sectors are the grouping of companies on the economic spectrum by similar characteristics. Economies are divided into four sectors. The primary sector involves the extraction and harvesting of natural resources from the Earth. The second sector encompasses processing, manufacturing and construction. The third sector provides services such as financial services, entertainment, and retail sales. Finally, the fourth sector is made up of intellectual pursuit.

These four economic sectors are divided into more detailed sectors based on companies' businesses. Standard and Poor's breaks the market into 11 sectors. Two of them (utilities and consumer staples) are said to be defensive sectors, while the remaining nine sectors are considered cyclical in nature. This distinction is important because defensive sector companies tend to perform well in down cycles because their product or services are always consumed. A full list of the 11 sectors is below:

TABLE 2 - ECONOMIC SECTORS
Basic Materials
Capital Goods
Communications Services
Consumer Cyclical
Consumer Staples
Energy
Financial
Health Care
Technology
Transportation
Utilities

Each of these sectors is made up of subsectors or industries. Industries comprise of companies with similar products or services. An example of the difference between sectors and industries is the following. The Technology sector is made up of several different industries including: Application Software, Business Solution and Services, Communication Equipment, Internet Providers Software, Hardware, and more. Industries will come and go but economic sectors are long lasting. The horse and buggy was once a major industry in the Transportation sector, but it does not exist in the manner it did in the 1800's.

Experts in the Market Place

Financial Experts who can serve you are called a variety of names depending on the type of help you need. Financial Advisors' main role is to manage your investment portfolio. Traditionally, they were paid a commission on the transactions in the account. However, more and more are paid based on the total amount of assets under their control, as well as the year-over-year growth of the assets under management.

Certified Financial Planners (CFPs) focus on developing the strategy around the portfolio, which includes asset allocation between cash, stocks and bonds. It also includes planning for life events such as marriage, children, education, retirement, and post life. Fund managers actively manage a fund or portfolio of funds based on predetermined strategies. Regardless of who gives you advice, manages your portfolio(s), or trades your account, ultimately, you are the responsible party, no matter how accountabilities are allocated.

Limits and IPOs

On December 8, 1999, I had been on the discount trading desk for six months. I joined the discount desk after working in Wachovia's Broker Direct for two years. Broker Direct was a full-service retail brokerage group. It was an exciting time as we were ending the 20th Century, and expectations around the new millennium were at an all time high. Technology stocks were soaring. Red Hat (RHT), a software company, went public three months earlier at $30 and began trading upwards of $150.

But, on this day, everyone was focused on VA Linux (LNUX). By association, the company was set to have a great initial public offering (IPO). As we prepared for the day, the demand for the stock surged. While the IPO price was set at $30, open market demand pushed it significantly higher.

One of the great things about being a discount broker is that you can see the full market. We could see the Bid and Ask for all trades in the system. So, we had a good feel of the market for LNUX.

Initial Public Offerings (IPOs) are the first sale of stock by a private company to the public. IPOs are often issued by smaller or younger companies seeking to raise capital. IPOs allow stakeholders to purchase shares of the company stock at a set price before they start trading in the market place.

As a broker, we always tell clients to put a limit order on trades when purchasing an IPO. A buy limit order sets the price at which a client will pay the most for a stock. So everyone on the desk was startled when we saw an open market order for 1,000 shares of LNUX. Brokers asked who put an open market order on an IPO. It was a new broker in Broker Direct. I knew the guy, so I called him. I told him to put a limit on the order. He stated the client wanted the stock regardless of the price. Since he would not listen, I called my old manager, but he was on vacation. I called the broker again, but he insisted he knew what he was doing. He would not change the trade. He told me the IPO was priced at $30, and the client stated he wanted in on this deal.

When LNUX finally started trading, it opened above $290 and reached a high of $320 before it closed at $263. The client's order was filled between $310 and $317 for a total average cost of roughly $313,500. The client did not have enough to cover the trade. It is clear that $31,350 is a lot different than the $313,500. We had to break the trade and take the loss. The broker lost his job. The client did not get the stock. The stock did not trade at the IPO price. As a matter of fact, the 700% increase in market price was a record. Interestingly, when investors realized that the company evaluation did not match, the shares fell well below its IPO price just one year later. Four years later, it traded below $6.

Summary

- Financial markets are comprised of submarket such as the stock market, bond market, futures market, spot market, etc.

- Investors view the market from several different perspectives including capitalization, categorization, and sectors and industries.

- Capitalization is grouping companies by their market capitalization or the company's price times shares outstanding.

- Categorization is grouping companies by their performance behavior over time. Companies may move through the categorization cycle as they mature.

- Sector and industry is grouping companies by the business model characteristics. There are roughly 11 economic sectors. Each sector is comprised of multiple industries.

- Financial experts have different names, depending on their areas of focus and skillset.

Popcorn Service!

So, I don't like movie theater or stadium popcorn. This fact has actually gotten me in trouble because it appears that I am cheap if I express that I don't want it. Apparently, eating popcorn is like having an intoxicating beverage; no one wants to eat it alone. I have a really good reason for my aversion to publically made popcorn. It started when I was in the seventh grade.

In junior high school, we raised money for ancillary sports activities by selling refreshments after school. We sold drinks, chips, candy and popcorn. I started volunteering in the seventh grade after Coach Carter asked me to participate. Initially, I only sold the items. We sold it year round out of a window in one of the classrooms. It was a great experience. I met different people from all three campuses (elementary, junior high, and high school).

One day, Coach Carter asked me why I never ate the popcorn. Everyone who volunteered could have their share of drinks because we poured by cups from liters. We could have all the popcorn we wanted. However, I would buy the candy bars or chips. I never ate the popcorn. So, when he asked me the question, in my seventh grade honesty, I blurted, "It's nasty!" As he prepared to make another batch, he looked at me and said, "You think you can do better, have at it." He then stormed out of the room. Honestly, the popcorn was extremely salty. I mean, it was so salty that it was deep orange in color. People cringed as they ate it. On top of that, too much was made at one time, so it would be cold when we sold it.

Thus began my popcorn making. I cleaned the pan of the excess salt. My goal was to make the popcorn buttery and lite. So, I added more butter and significantly less salt. Over time I began to make popcorn that was bright yellow and slightly salty. We began to sell more popcorn. I began to eat more popcorn.

Now, when I see how people make popcorn, I reflect back to my junior high school experience. I just believe if you are going to sell a product or service, you should do it with care. You should do it as if you are going to consume or use it yourself.

Things impacting the Investment Tools

Unlike many investors, I have had the opportunity to work in an equity research department, a brokerage unit, and an institutional investment group. These experiences have given me insight on dynamics that influence the market place, such as the impact of investors' behaviors, investment firms' characteristics, and technology.

Up to this point, we talked about the investment vehicles and products that are exchanged in the market place. However, the market place is made up of investment firms, investors and the technology that connects them. The landscape has changed drastically over the years with deregulation, socioeconomic changes, and advancement in the Internet. If we were in OZ, these would be the things behind the curtain that impact the market place.

Deregulation—Glass-Steagall Act of 1933

The Glass-Steagall Act – GSA- (named after Senator Carter Glass and Senator Henry Steagall) prohibited banks from participating in investment banking business. It was a direct result from the 1929 Market Crash where more than 5,000 banks collapsed and caused the Great Depression. The Glass-Steagall Act had two major objectives: to restore confidence in the U.S. banking system and to sever the link between commercial and investment banking. The reason for this separation was the belief that more conservative commercial banks were negatively impacted by the excessive level of risk taken by investment banks.

Over the next 60 years, changing regulations and legislation weakened GSA. Finally, it was completely repealed in 1999 during the President Clinton Administration. It is worth noting that commercial banks began purchasing investment companies in the 1970s. Repeal of GSA and other deregulation laws have changed the landscape of the market place.

Deregulation has led to a consolidation in the brokerage industry. Banking holding companies now own many of the retail brokerage firms. With this change in the landscape, brokerage firms have changed their focus to higher net-worth customers ($250,000 and higher). Financial advisors are more asset gatherers than traditional brokers. Firms focus more on fee-based products instead of commission-based trading. They also require more cross sales of traditional banking products.

Investor Behavior and Technology

While deregulation changed the landscape of the banks and investment firms, investor behaviors have changed because of the expectations of more and faster access to information for decision making. These expectations have been heightened with new and ever changing technology.

In the early 1990s, information was still somewhat limited and slow in dissemination. The personal computer was in its infancy as well as software packages and financial companies that supplied financial data to brokerage firms. The potential of the Internet was beginning to be realized. Yet, it could take three to six weeks for information about a company to be fully reflected in the market place.

At the same time, the investor profile continued to improve. Disposable and investable income grew at a significant rate, as the tide of prosperity lifted the upper and middle classes. Baby-boomers increased productivity and profit margins of companies. The number of individuals with investment accounts increased. Self-directed retirement accounts increased. The average age of the investor was 58. The average portfolio size was $174,000 in investable assets. Investors tend to have multiple accounts at different investment firms. Investors chose the do-it-yourself approach, as trust in financial advisors continued to fall.

Technology's first major impact was the development of "Book-Entry" holdings. Prior to the 1970s, the majority of stocks and bonds were delivered to the owner in physical form (stock or bond certificates). Many bonds were also in "Bearer" form which meant that whoever held the bonds were entitled to the principal and interest. The holder would clip the interest coupons and deliver them to their broker or administrator of the bond for payment. As you can imagine, this was an extremely challenging process to handle and the safety and security of ensuring the true owner was represented and paid was daunting.

In 1973 the Depository Trust Company (DTC) was created to reduce cost and provide clearing and settlement efficiencies by making "book-entry" changes to securities ownership. DTC provided securities movement for net settlements and settlement between custodian banks and broker dealers. With book-entry, the owner's name of the securities is held at the brokerage firm. The securities are held at DTC in the name of the brokerage firm. True owners were represented and physical securities held by shareholders were reduced or eradicated.

A major impact of book-entry is trade settlement. Traditionally, trade settlement or the time to deliver the security and money for a purchase/sell was five business days. In 1998, trade settlement decreased from five to three days. Thus, you will hear trade plus 3 or "T+3". However, with the connectivity of bank-side and investment-side accounts, investors must have the proceeds to pay for purchases the day of trade. Sellers must have the shares in the account to sell. Although trade settlement technically is T+3, in actuality it is same-day settlement.

Technology has also changed the method and the timing of how information flows to the market place. Electronic distribution has significantly reduced the cycle time of information. It also has given the investor more control of their accounts and trading capabilities.

Summary

- Investors have different paths to entering the financial marketplace.
- Three key things that have impacted the financial marketplace are deregulation, technology and investors' behavior.
- Deregulation has changed the landscape because of the consolidation of banks and brokerage firms. It also has changed the way securities are processed and trade settlement.
- With deregulation, investment firms have changed their structure and their market focus.
- Technology has decreased the information distribution cycle time. It has also given the investor access to more information. It allows the investor the ability to make trades.

Investment Strategies

So, the goal of this book is to:
- Explore the psychology of money
- Understand the products and vehicles of the market place
- Develop investment strategies

We started this discussion with the "Wizard of Oz" analogy, which tells the journey Dorothy took to find her way back to Kansas. She had ups and downs, but along her journey, she met people to help her and she learned a lot about herself. Some things she did with her new friends; others she had to do herself. This will be your experience as you move through or continue your investment management journey.

So far, we have talked about the value of money, investment products, investment vehicles and grouping of companies. We also talked about how deregulation, technology and customer behaviors continue to impact the investment world. Now, we start the journey of finding value in the market place.

The Oz analogy shows how the investment marketplace is not as mystic as it seems. We have examined the tools and discussed the knowledge one needs to navigate the marketplace. Now, we turn our focus to the investment strategies that consist of three areas: Investor's

Profile, Building the Portfolio, and Performance Evaluation. This process focuses on developing a customized strategy for each investor. The following is an outline of considerations:

The basic assumption going forward is that financial resources are available for investment.

The Investment Profile

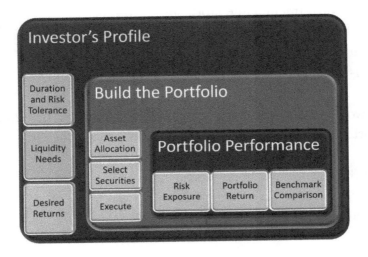

Often you will hear investing is a combination of art and science. It is rightly so that the art comes first. In professional and personal investing, the process begins with the investor profile. The profile is the foundation of the investment management process. Each stroke on the profile canvass is shaped by answers to the questionnaire. Changes throughout life impact the profile and investment decisions. The investment profile has three main areas: duration and risk tolerance, liquidity needs, and desired returns.

Investment Profile

- Duration – How long do you want to invest?
- Risk – How much risk can you tolerate?

- Liquidity – How much access to cash do you need?
- Returns – How much do you expect to make or grow your portfolio?

Duration – Investment Time Horizon
- Short-term 1 to 3 years
- Medium-term 4 to 9 years
- Long-term over 10 years

It is worth noting that these are standard guidelines. Investment time horizons change throughout the investor's life-cycle and events.

Risk – What is your aversion to risk?
- Risk & reward
- Volatility in price
- Lose of investment

It is important for the investor to understand the link between risk and reward. The greater the desired reward, the more risk is assumed by the investor. It may be difficult to achieve investment objectives without the willingness and ability to take on the risk of losing the total amount of the investment. Risk can be viewed from the allocation between cash, bonds, and stocks.

TABLE 3 - RISK BASED ON ASSET ALLOCATION			
	Conservative Risk	Moderate Risk	Aggressive Risk
Investment Product	High Liquidity	Moderate Liquidity	Low Liquidity
Cash	70%	15%	10%
Bonds	20%	55%	20%
Stocks	10%	30%	70%

Note: See Asset Allocation Models in the Appendix for an expanded view of allocation models.

Risk also can be viewed by the exposure to individual investments.

Example 1. Allocation and Risk Management

An investor has $100,000 to invest. The first step is to determine the mix between cash, bonds, and stocks. The investor selects an aggressive strategy thus 70% of the $100,000 will be invested in stocks. The next step is to determine how much of the $70,000 will be invested in a single stock.

The investor decides a standard invest in an individual stock will be 3%, or $2,100. If the stock is trading at $10 then the investor would purchase 210 shares (2,100 / 10).

If the investor really likes the stock, 5%, or $3,500 will be invested. If the stock is trading at $5 per share, then the investor would purchase 700 shares (3,500 / 5).

If the investor is not really sure about the stock but would take a chance, then a 2%, or $1,440, stake would be taken. If the share is trading at $2 then the investor would purchase 720 shares (1,400/2).

Liquidity – How quickly can one get to the cash?
- Type of investment vehicle
- How much in cash
- When is the cash needed

Liquidity is important because it impacts the type of investment vehicle that can be used and asset allocation. For example, tax advantage vehicles may have negative consequences if you draw the money outside of certain preset conditions. Additionally, if the investor has a time horizon of less than a year in which the cash will be needed, it reduces the level of risk the investor should assume. The type of investment product is also impacted by the need of liquidity. If the liquidity need is high, products that are easily converted to cash should be purchased. [Refer to Table 3]

Returns – How are you going to earn the money?
- Growth – Price appreciation
- Income – Dividend and/or interest
- Total return – Growth plus income

Build the Portfolio

Once the investor profile has been completed, the science begins. Building the portfolio incorporates "brain and courage" to identify and buy the investments that aligns to the investor's profile. Some investors need help with this while others are capable of doing it themselves. The elements needed to build the portfolio are asset allocation, selecting securities, executing the order and evaluating performance.

Asset Allocation
- Balance between cash, stock and bonds
- Allocating between conservative and aggressive investments
- Amount invested in individual securities
- Select a benchmark

Selecting Securities
- Different investment products
- Divide equity portion between different sectors and market capitalization
- Determine the portion of bond investment between government and corporate debt

Execute
- Research the company
- Determine which type of securities you will buy (stock or bond)
- Determine a fair buy price
- Determine a fair sale price

Performance Evaluation
- Yield
- Return – Total Return
- Benchmark

Yield measures the income on gains for owning an investment during a specific period of time. It is usually expressed as a percentage and is calculated by dividing the income by the investment price. Bonds, cash, certificates of deposits and most mutual funds usually have yields. However, a stock will only have a yield if it pays a dividend.

Return measures the appreciation or depreciation of an investment over a specific period of time. It is derived:

Change in Value/Investment Amount = Percentage Return

Or

New Value/Old Value − 1 = Percentage Return

Total Return, considered the most accurate measure of return, sums the change in value plus income divided by cost of the investment. It is calculated:

Total Return %= (Change in value plus income)/Investment Amount

Or

Total Return %= (New Value + Income)/Old Value − 1

Example 2 – Returns Calculation

An investor buys a stock for $10 dollars at the beginning of the year. The stock pays a $1.00 annual dividend. The dividend is paid out quarterly. By the end of the year, the stock has grown to $15.

Yield% = $1.00 Dividend / $10 purchase price * 100% = $1.00 / $10 *100% = 10%

Return% = (New Value / Old Value −1) * 100% = ($15 / $10 − 1) * 100% = 50%

Total Return% = ((New Value + Income) / Old Value − 1) * 100% = (($15 + $1) / $10 − 1) * 100% = 60%

Tracking Performance
- Daily Tracking
- Monthly Tracking
- Quarterly Tracking
- Annual Tracking

Benchmark Comparison

One of the key elements of building a portfolio is determining how you will measure success. Two measures are absolute performance and relative performance. Absolute performance asks the question: does the portfolio's ending balance exceed the beginning balance? Relative performance asks the question: how does the portfolio's absolute performance compare to similar portfolios? A benchmark should be selected in the portfolio development phase of the Investment Process. There are many benchmarks to select from depending on your level of risk and reward profile. The benchmark can also help you select the securities to achieve your objective. On a periodic basis (monthly, quarterly, annually) your portfolio can be compared to the benchmark to determine relative performance. It gives insight on if any adjustments to your portfolio are needed to get better results.

Summary

- The investment process consists of understanding the investor's profile, building the portfolio, and performance evaluation.

- Investor Profile gives insight on one's investment preferences, including risk tolerance, liquidity, and expected returns.

- Building the portfolio consists of identifying the asset allocation, selecting the securities to purchase and determining how to execute your strategy.

- Once the portfolio and strategy have been implemented, periodic performance evaluation helps to keep you on target or adjust to changing market and company events.

- Some investors' primary strategy is price appreciation (growth in the stock), while others focus on yield (interest or dividend income). Others desire a total return strategy that is price appreciation plus a good interest or dividend yield.

Portfolio Management

A Portfolio is a collection of assets. If you have any combination of real estate, cars, clothes, etc., you have a portfolio of assets. A monetary investment portfolio is a basket of investments such as cash, bonds and stocks. The Market is a portfolio of cash, bonds, stocks and their derivatives from which an investor will select. The market portfolio is dynamic.

Our goal is to search for value in the market place. We do so by following the investment process flow. There are fundamental assumptions about the market as we build our portfolio and search for value in the market.

Market Assumptions:
- Investors evaluate portfolios by looking at the variance and expected returns over a one-period horizon (for example: year-over-year).
- Investors, when given a choice between two otherwise identical portfolios, will choose the one with the higher expected return.
- Investors are risk-averse.
- Individual assets are infinitely divisible.
- There is a risk-free rate at which an investor may either lend or borrow money.
- Taxes and transaction costs are negligible.
- Assume all information is available at the same time to all investors.

Separation Theorem

The Separation Theorem states that the optimal combination of risky assets for an investor can be determined without any knowledge of the investor's preferences toward risk and return. In other words, the investor's decision to invest can be separated from the decision of what to buy. Additionally, the investment product and combination of investment products can be grouped exclusive of the investor. When you enter the supermarket, the products are already on the shelves for selection. The same is true in the financial marketplace. While intimately connected, the decision to invest and decision on what to buy are driven by different things:

The decision to invest is based primarily on socioeconomic factors such as:

- Risk Aversion
- Economic Climate
- Financial Situation
- Family Matters
- Fear
- Greed

The decision of what to buy is based primarily on market and security analysis factors such as:

- Risk Aversion
- Asset Allocation-mix of cash, stock, bonds
- Life Cycle
- Reason for Investing
- Expectations!

Portfolio management encompasses the separation theorem to reflect the investor's willingness to invest and ability to select products from the market place.

Sometimes, investors don't have the willingness to invest in the market for several reasons. These investors tend to stay on the sidelines or utilize the least risky investment vehicles and products. Other investors have the willingness to invest but lack the ability to select from the market. So they either sit on the sidelines, learn by trial, or find someone to help them. Yet other investors have the willingness to invest and ability to execute their investment strategy and manage their portfolio on their own.

If you are a part of the first group of investors, hopefully this book helps you find your way. If you are a part of the second group of investors, we will give insight on what to look for when considering an investment advisor. Finally, if you are a DIY investor, this book will provide a roadmap to follow.

Execution of the Plan

Financial Advisor versus Do-It-Yourself Investing

Selecting a Financial Advisor

As mentioned earlier, financial advisors focus more on individuals with investable assets of $250,000 and higher. While the baby-boomer tends to have higher amounts, the average investor has approximately $70,000 in investable assets in three accounts across two different financial institutions. Because of this gap in target market and the average investor, it puts more responsibility on the investor to understand how to interact with the financial advisor. These are things to consider when selecting a financial advisor:

- Does the advisor have any negative reviews?
- How well does the broker know the market?
- Does the advisor seek to provide expertise about the market?
- Do you gel with broker?
- How much does it cost to utilize the services?
- What are the array of services offered by the broker and the company?

Once you have selected the financial advisor, you need to understand how the advisor operates. The following are things you need to understand about your advisor:

- Usage of individual stocks/bonds versus mutual funds as a solution
- Time management of meetings including phone calls
- Other services at your disposal

- Market insight and investment advice.

Regardless of who is giving you advice, managing your portfolio or trading your account, you ultimately are the responsible party, no matter how accountabilities are allocated. The investor should exercise prudence. The investor should understand:

- How the advisor is paid?
- Fees schedules (annual fees versus commission based trading)
- Is there a higher commission for selling certain products?
- Watch for "churning" (excessive trading to generate commission)

The advisor acts as an agent for the firm where they work even though they may go to market for you. Therefore, careful attention should be paid to how the advisor is compensated. While the advisor should work on your behalf, they also are concerned about their own well-being. Understanding how they are paid will help you in understanding what you should expect from the advisor.

Often you will hear the phrase sophisticated investor. Most people believe it describes an investor who understands the market extremely well. However, it is far from the truth. A sophisticated investor is someone who can sustain a huge loss without significantly impacting hers/his financial situation. However, a prudent investor is an individual who make decisions based on sound research and discipline.

Summary

- The market is a portfolio of assets from which products are selected and added to individual portfolios. There are market assumptions when selecting securities.

- Separation Theorem states that the investor's decision to invest can be separated from the decision of what to buy. The decision to invest is based on socioeconomic factors while what to buy is built on market and security analysis factors.

- The decision to invest can be broken down to the investor's willingness to invest and ability to select. The willingness to invest includes variables such as financing, lifecycle, or emotional perspectives. The ability to select includes market knowledge and security analysis.

- Investors fall along the spectrum of individuals' willingness and ability to invest. Where the individual falls on this continuum determines if they are in the market, seek help from an advisor, or do it themselves.

- Investors who seek an advisor should understand the advisor's background, all the services at their disposal, and the cost for their products and services.

Do-It-Yourself Investing

While the baby-boomer generation investment balances are higher, on average individual investors have three accounts across two investments firms with an average of $70,000 in investable assets. Some investors have four or five accounts with roughly $10,000 to $20,000 in each of them. What I have found is that a lot of investors usually open accounts without really knowing or understanding why they open them. Remember, the vehicle is sometimes more important than what is inside because the vehicle has to protect what is inside.

Many individuals are told to open an IRA account for 401(k) rollovers when they leave their employer. Some people open an account because a friend told them to do so or perhaps they are trying to follow television or online, "how-to" sites. There are also individuals who let their investments stay with their former employer. So, some people have investments in multiple accounts, different firms, and multiple former employers. Now, that can be a challenge to manage.

My suggestion is to follow the professional method of operations. The determination and declaration of your motivation to be in the market is the first step in building your strategy. It may change over time, but it is important to determine the ultimate goal for the account. How will you measure success? If possible, consolidate and aggregate your investments based on your investment goals. Please revisit the Investment Strategies section to ensure you understand the process and its impact on your success in the market place.

As we stated, "Do-It-Yourself" investors have the willingness and ability to make and execute their investment decisions. While there are a lot of investment strategies, the basic elements are the same.

Whether it is a financial advisor, portfolio manager, or DIY investor, they all need research sources, risk profile, and a buy-sell criteria.

Technology regulatons,and legislation have had a major impact on the investment landscape. Every investment firm offers some research capabilities for their clients. However, the DIY investor should have at least two sources to research companies. Some investment firms follow companies because they have or want a financial relationship with the company. Sometimes this may cause a conflict of interest, as the investment firm may be resistant to write a negative report. Examples of research sources are research reports from investment firms, news articles from the firm's website, and other online information. Multiple sources can give a broader perspective on the company and its activities and potential.

Establishing a risk profile is key to the investment process. The risk profile describes the level of risk the investor is willing to accept for a certain level of reward. Asset preservation, or minimizing loss, is the first aspect of risk management. The second aspect of risk management is asset allocation. Asset allocation is how investable dollars are divided between investment products. Diversification is the investment based on industries and sectors. It takes roughly 10 to 12 investment positions to achieve optimal investment diversification.

Finally, the purchase amount of individual investment is critical to the risk management process and establishing your risk profile. Each investment has a potential of appreciating above your expectations or depreciating to zero. Therefore, the purchase amount should represent a percentage of your investable assets where the loss of one investment would not substantially impact your portfolio.

The Selection Process

DIY Investors have the willingness to invest and the ability to select from the market place. The ability to select includes the understanding of the fundamental analysis we presented in the Investment Products chapter. The selection process starts with screening the Market for potential companies to analyze. Top down and bottom up are two approaches to the selection process.

The top-down approach begins with looking at the big picture. It looks at the drivers of the economy as well as geopolitical and socioeconomic activities. Once an understanding of the impacts of the economy is determined, the selection process begins by looking for the best performing sectors and industries. The next step is to look for the best performing companies within those industries. A smaller group of companies is created. Fundamental analysis is applied to determine which companies are considered undervalued, fairly valued or overvalued.

The bottom-up approach starts with a single company. The company can be chosen based on news, word of mouth, etc. This approach focuses more on determining if the company is the best selection by comparing it to other companies in its industry and the market. It is also compared to other companies in other industries to determine if it is the best allocation of your investment dollars.

The top-down approach creates small groups from which to select, while the bottom-up approach determines if the known company should be purchased. In both methods, the investor should remember that a stock or bond purchase is an investment in the company. Therefore, there are three fundamental criteria to consider when investing in a company: the product, management team, and valuation of the stock.

When investing in a company, the belief is that the product or service the company offers satisfies a need, and it is something that can be sold to a large group. There also is a belief that the product or service has pricing power. The community that buys the product or service will do so even with small price increases over time. The company can enhance the products or service and increase the sales. Alternatively, changes in the products or services could have negative impact of sales. It is worth noting that it is acceptable to purchase certain companies' products or services but not invest in those companies. The opposite of this is also true.

The management team is another major criterion when selecting a company. The team is responsible for everything from product management to strategic decisions on how to run the business. Marketing the product, financial decisions, and community impact all help in the success of a business. A great product in itself will not make a business profitable and successful over the long-term. It takes a great management team to leverage the success of the product to create a company in which to invest. Changes in the management team can have enormous impact on the company. The DIY investor must pay attention to the impact management has on the company and its products.

Finally, the DIY investor should have an understanding of the drivers of the security performance. There is a plethora of fundamental calculations that can be used to evaluate the status of the company and the performance of the stock. Depending on the security these ratios will help determine if a company should be purchased, held, sold or avoided. While we covered valuation earlier, we will reiterate a few of the ratios:

- ROI – Return of Investment
- ROA – Return on Assets
- D/E – Debt to Equity
- Interest Coverage Ratio
- EPS – Earnings per share
- P/E Ratio – Price to Earnings Ratio

These are just a few of the many calculations that can be used to evaluate a company and its stock. The Valuation Table in the appendix lists Balance Sheet, Income Statement, Overall Efficiency, and Market Performance Ratios and what they measure. The DIY investor will have to determine their own criteria and discipline when building their portfolio. These calculations are then applied to the subset of companies or they can be used to create a subset of companies to evaluate.

The Selection Compass

Once the filtering and analysis have been completed it is time to take action. For some, this action point is paralyzing while for others it just simply pushing a button. The action phase of the selection process is like a compass. One can buy, hold, sell, or avoid. Sometimes the decision is not as clear as one would like. Emotions sometime play a major role on how the investor operates in the action phase.

When to Buy

The ultimate motivator in the investment market place is to make a profit on the investment. There are only two options: buy low—sell high or sell high—buy low. Some investors believe receiving income in the form of dividends or interest helps to offset this simple strategy. The second motivator is preservation of capital. No one wants to lose their money.

A target sell price for the security should be identified before it is purchased. This target sell price can be an absolute dollar value or it can be an expected percentage growth. The investor should buy when they believe one or more of the following is true:

- Analysis show the company is undervalued and it is reflected in the price of the security.
- The security is fairly valued, but momentum in the market place show that it may move pass the target sell price.
- Research and analysis show a future event may have a significant positive impact on the product or service; or on the management team.

It is worth noting, making a buying decision simply because of a friend told you about the security may not be a prudent decision. The valuation for you will be different than your friend especially if the security has performed well between the time your friend bought it and when he/she told you.

When to hold

So you made the decision to buy the security. You are now committed to this security for some period of time. If you purchased it based on the fundamental analysis the popularity of the the company might be low, company sales might be off, or there is a major change in management. You may have purchased a little too soon. Knowing how long to hold the stock is tricky. You have identified the target sell price. In general, you should hold the security as long as one or more of the following are true:

- The fundamental analysis shows the performance of the company and subsequently the security still holds true for your designated time horizon.
- There are no significant negative changes in management or the product or service.
- The price of the security does not fall below your designated loss point. Usually this is around a 10 to 20 percent loss.
- Your personal financial needs do not require liquidation.
- The security has not reached your target sell price.

The decision to continue to hold a security can become extremely emotional. The security may experience lackluster performance while the market is performing well but the fundamentals say hold. The entire market may tank for unknown reasons thus impacting the purchased security. It sometimes will take intestinal fortitude and discipline to maintain a hold position in light of market moves or company news.

When to Sell

The decision to buy has been made with a target sell price. But the decision to sell is not as simple as pushing the button. As mentioned, the ultimate motivator is to make a profit. In general, the investor may sell based on one or a combination of the following:

- The security has reached the investor's target sell price.
- Significant negative news or information have come to light about the management team, product or service or overall company performance.
- The price of the security has fallen below your designated loss point. Usually this is around a 10 to 20 percent loss.

However, other factors may impact the decision to not sell. For instance, the investor may like the dividend or interest payment from the security, new research suggest the original target price should be upwardly adjusted, or there is no alternative investment option.

When to Avoid

Preservation of capital is the first rule of investment. Consistently losing money will erode your investment portfolio as well as damage your selection process. Sometimes it's difficult to distinguish between a value trap and a value buy. Some stocks may look attractive depending on market conditions. The selection process is used to determine if it's prudent to take the plunge. Beyond the buy, hold, and sell decision, sometimes it is wiser to avoid the investment. Some reasons investments might be avoided:

- Lack of understanding the company's product or services
- Companies that have too much debt
- Companies whose break-even costs are too high
- Companies with consistent poor management decisions
- Social conscience issues
- Stock is in a significant downtrend
- Some penny stocks

These are just a few reasons to avoid some investment opportunities. The decision to avoid is based on your criteria and discipline. Therefore, the investment's performance may be irrelevant.

Summary

- DIY investing is growing with the aging of the population. The average investor has three investment accounts worth $70,000 across two investment firms.

- DIY investors should develop a strategy based on their investor profile and risk tolerance.

- Asset allocation is the distribution of investable dollars between investment products. Diversification is the investment based on industries and sectors. It takes roughly 10 to 12 investment positions to achieve optimal investment diversification.

- The selection process starts with screening the Market for potential companies to analyze. Top down and bottom up are two approaches investors use to screen the Market.

- There are three fundamental criteria to consider when investing in a company: the product, management team, and valuation of the stock.

- Once the fundamental selection process is completed, the buy, hold, sell or avoid decision has to be made.

Conclusion

Dorothy's journey began with a desire to get back home. Along the way, she met witches, munchkins, and other scary things. She also found help from a scarecrow, tinman, and lion. She discovered that the Wizard wasn't as big nor as scary as people made him out to be.

Dorothy thought she had found her way home by sharing a hot-air balloon ride with the wizard. But she was left behind. When she thought she was at her wits end, someone told her the answer had always been there. SSo, with a click of her shoes and her motivational declaration, she found her way to her desired destination. "There's no place like home", she found her way to her desired destination.

Similar to Dorothy, you may find yourself on a financial journey. Your motivational declaration has set you on a path that can change your life. There will be challenges along the way, but you now have the knowledge and insight to move forward. You might have set backs on your journey. There will be learning and growing pains. However, staying focused will get you to your destination.

The market is not as scary as one may believe. There are many resources to help you down your path. The willingness to invest is the driving force that will energize your learning. The ability to select investment products can be improved by finding support from the right person and studying the methods in this book.

Wyndon

Appendices

Valuation Table

This table details ratios used to evaluate company and stock performance. They can be used to create subsets of companies from a top down selection process. It can also use to analyze single companies from a bottom up selection process.

TABLE 4 - VALUATION RATIOS		
Balance Sheet Ratios		
Ratio	Calculation	Meaning
Current Ratio	Current Assets / Current Liabilities	Measures solvency: The number of dollars in Current Assets for every $1 in Current Liabilities.
Quick Ratio	Cash + Accounts Receivable / Current Liabilities	Measures liquidity: The number of dollars in Cash and Accounts Receivable for each $1 in Current Liabilities.
Debt-to-Net worth	Total Liabilities / Net Worth	Measures financial risk: The number of dollars of Debt owed for every $1 in Net Worth

Income Statement Ratios		
Ratio	Calculation	Meaning
Gross Margin	Gross Profit / Sales	Measures profitability at the Gross Profit level: The number of dollars of Gross Margin produced for every $1 of Sales.
Net Profit Margin	Net Profit Before Tax / Sales	Measures profitability at the Net Profit level: The number of dollars Net Profit for every dollar of sales

Overall Efficiency Ratios		
Ratio	Calculation	Meaning
Sales-To Assets	Sales / Total Assets	Measures efficiency of total assets in generating sales
Return of Assets	Net Profit Before Tax / Total Assets	Measure efficiency of Total Assets in generating Net Profit

Market Performance Ratios		
Ratio	**Calculation**	**Meaning**
Price-to-Earnings	Current Market Price / Earnings Per Share	Measure how much an investor is willing to pay for future earnings
Price-to-Book	Current Market Price / Book Value Per Share	Measures how much an investor is willing to pay over the solvency value of the company
Dividend Yield	Dividend Payment / Current Market Price	Measures how much cash flow you are getting for each dollar invested in an equity position
Bond Yield	Bond Interest Payment / Current Bond Price	Measures how much cash flow you are getting for each dollar invested in an equity position
Beta	Calculated by Regression Analysis	Measures the sensitivity of a securities price swing to movements in the overall market.

Asset Allocation Models

The following charts are an expanded view of asset allocations models discussed in Table 3 Risk Based on Asset Allocation

* Source: Wachovia Securities

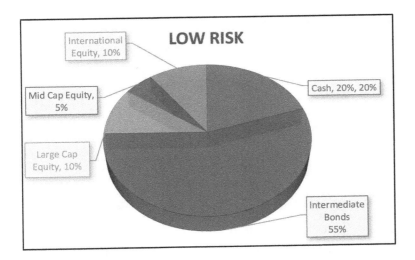

	Low Risk
Cash	20%
Intermediate Bonds	55%
Large Cap Equity	10%
Mid Cap Equity	5%
International Equity	10%

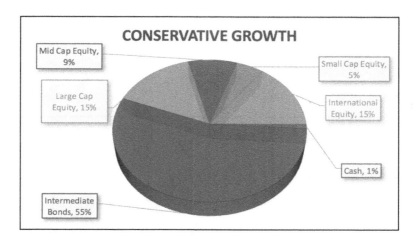

	Conservative Growth
Cash	1%
Intermediate Bonds	55%
Large Cap Equity	15%
Mid Cap Equity	9%
Small Cap Equity	5%
International Equity	15%

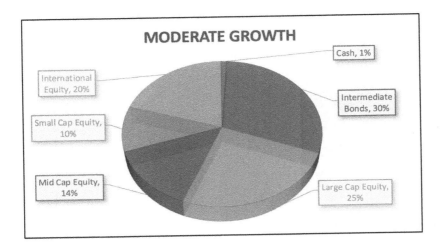

	Moderate Growth
Cash	1%
Intermediate Bonds	30%
Large Cap Equity	25%
Mid Cap Equity	14%
Small Cap Equity	10%
International Equity	20%

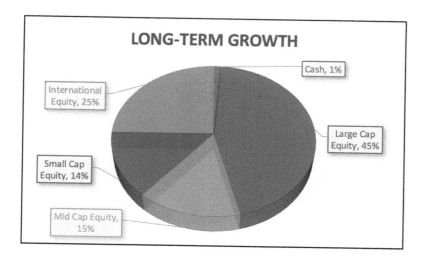

	Long-Term Growth
Cash	1%
Large Cap Equity	45%
Mid Cap Equity	15%
Small Cap Equity	14%
International Equity	25%

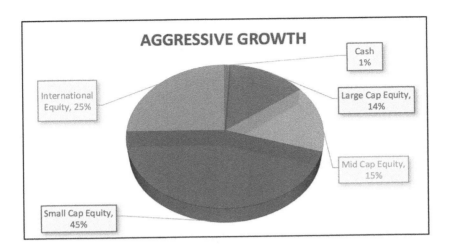

	Aggressive Growth
Cash	1%
Large Cap Equity	14%
Mid Cap Equity	15%
Small Cap Equity	45%
International Equity	25%

Sources and Description of Data

Money Psychology

History of Greed by David E. Y. Sarna, published by Wiley & Sons, copyright 2010

The Six Living Generation in America by Dr. Jill Novak, University of Phoenix, Texas A&M University, marketingteacher.com
http://www.marketingteacher.com/the-six-living-generations-in-america/

Boomers to Millennials: Generational Attitudes
by: Cara Newman, YOUNG MONEY Editor
http://finance.youngmoney.com/careers/
boomers-to-millennials-generational-attitudes/

Millennial Generation's Non-Negotiables: Money, Fame and Image
Alice G. Walton
http://www.forbes.com/sites/alicegwalton/2012/03/19/
millennial-generations-non-negotiables-money-fame-and-image/

How the Great Recession Changed Generations' Money Views by Andrea Murad
http://www.foxbusiness.com/personal-finance/2012/04/26/
how-great-recession-changed-generations-money-views/

How Nature Vs. Nurture Impact Your Spending Habits by Richard Barrington
http://www.huffingtonpost.com/richard-barrington/nature-nurture-and-saving_b_751780.html

LOVE AND MONEY IN AMERICA by LearnVest/TD Ameritrade
http://www.learnvest.com/wp-content/uploads/2013/01/LV_tda-white-paper.pdf

Investment Tools and Investment Strategies

Investments 2nd Edition by Zvi Bodie, Alex Kane, and Alan J. Marcus, published by Irwin, copyright 1993

The Investment Answer, Learning to Manage Your Money & Protect Your Financial Future, Daniel C. Goldie, CFA, CFP & Gordon S. Murray, published by Business Plus, copyright 2011

Analysis For Financial Management 5th Edition by Robert C. Higgins published Irwin McGraw-Hill, copyright 1998

Investment Analysis and Portfolio Management 6th Edition by Frank K. Reilly and Keith C. Brown, published by The Dryden Press, copyright 2000

The Citi Commonsense Money Guide for Real People, Edited by Dara Duquay, published by Citigroup, copyright 2007

The Asset Allocation Investment Process by Wachovia Securities copyright 2003

Picking Your First Broker by Jonas Elmerraji, Investopedia.com
http://www.investopedia.com/articles/younginvestors/06/firstbroker.asp

Picking a Broker by Motley Fool Staff, Fool.com
http://www.fool.com/investing/brokerage/picking-a-broker.aspx

Acknowledgment

I would like to thank all of my family and friends who have supported me through this process. Your help has been sincerely appreciated.

Though we teach collectively, we enlighten individually.